Me, Intentionally

Me, Intentionally

7 BIBLICAL STRATEGIES FOR GODLY SUCCESS

Dr. Stephanie L. Foster

All Scripture quotations, unless otherwise indicated, are taken from the Holy Bible, New International Version®, NIV ®. Copyright © 1973, 1978, 1984, 2011 by Biblica, Inc.™ Used by permission of Zondervan. All rights reserved worldwide. www.zondervan.com The "NIV" and "New International Version" are trademarks registered in the United States Patent and Trademark Office by Biblica, Inc.™

Scripture quotations marked (AMP) are taken from the Amplified Bible, Copyright © 1954, 1958, 1962, 1964, 1965, 1987 by The Lockman Foundation. Used by permission.

Scripture quoted by permission. Quotations designated (NET) are from the NET Bible ®copyright © 1996-2006 by Biblica Studies Press, L.L.C. http://netbible.com All rights reserved.

Scripture quotations marked (CEV) are from the Contemporary English Version Copyright © 1991, 1992, 1995 by American Bible Society, Used by Permission.

Scripture quotations from The Authorized (King James) Version. Rights in the Authorized Version in the United Kingdom are vested in the Crown. Reproduced by permission of the Crown's patentee, Cambridge University Press.

Scriptures and additional materials quoted are from the Good News Bible ©1994 published by the Bible Societies/HarperCollins Publishers Ltd UK, Good News Bible © American Bible Society 1966, 1971, 1976, 1992. Used with permission.

New Living Translation (NLT) Holy Bible. New Living Translation copyright ©1996 by Tyndale Charitable Trust. Used by permission of Tyndale House Publishers.

Scripture taken from THE MESSAGE. Copyright ©1993, 1994, 1995, 1996, 2000, 2001, 2002. Used by permission of NavPress Publishing Group.

Scripture quotations marked (ESV) are from the ESV Bible (The Holy Bible, English Standard Version), copyright ©2001 by Crossway, a publishing ministry of Good News Publishers. Used by permission. All rights reserved.

Scripture quotations marked TPT are taken from Proverbs: Wisdom from Above, The Passion Translation ®, copyright ©2014. Used by permission of Broadstreet Publishing Group, LLC, Racine, Wisconsin, USA. All rights reserved.

This book is intended only as an informative guide for those wishing to learn about behavior modification. The reader assumes all responsibility for the consequences of any actions taken based on the information presented in this book. The information presented in this book is based upon the author's research and experience. Every attempt has been made to ensure the presented information is accurate, however, the author cannot accept liability for any errors that may exist.

Copyright ©2015 Dr. Stephanie L. Foster. All rights reserved. No part of this book may be reproduced or transmitted in any form or by any means, electronic or mechanical, including photocopying, recording, or by any information storage and retrieval system, without the written permission of the author, except for the inclusion of brief quotations in a review.
ISBN: 1516948416
ISBN 13: 9781516948413

Dedication

I dedicate this book to my mother who instilled in me the belief that I could achieve anything I put my mind to and who showed me how, time and time again, to stand up to anyone and anything that dared to impede my progress. She is a trailblazer who birthed three biological children and numerous spiritual children while serving God as a proud Army wife, consummate business professional, inspirational educator, and phenomenal matriarch. Though she is now present with God, her love spans the dimensions of space, reminding me of her priorities: God, family, the joy of life, and the necessity of giving. I'm grateful to God for so many things...primary among them being Mary's daughter.

Acknowledgments

Saying and giving thanks is so important to me. It reminds me that I am not alone. I am surrounded by a robust support structure that empowers me to be my best self and boldly approach life. I am so grateful for my God, my husband, my family, my friends, my church, my colleagues, and my mentors. You are my strength, support, and encouragement.

In having you, I am most richly blessed!

Table of Contents

Acknowledgments · ix

Foreword: Godly Success Explained · · · · · · · · · · xiii

Foundation: God has A Good Plan for My Life! · xix

Chapter 1 Keep First Things First! · 1

Chapter 2 Set the Atmosphere! · 5

Chapter 3 Be Grateful! · 9

Chapter 4 Do It Today! · 14

Chapter 5 Complete Something! · 18

Chapter 6 Connect Meaningfully! · · · · · · · · · · · · · · · · · · · 22

Chapter 7	Do Something Good!	26
	Action Plan	31
	Reflections	35
	References	39
	Prayer of Salvation	41
	About the Author	43

Foreword: Godly Success Explained

Success. All around us, so many voices vie for our attention in telling us what success is and how to get it. Images fill our minds, alternatively affirming or disparaging our progress in "living the good life" or "making it". Heroes and role models seem to dance through life with each day bringing more acclaim and privilege. At times, we learn of their struggles, particularly if their excesses take destructive turns. Nonetheless, the mainstream thought of "get all you can, can all you get, and sit on the can" drives many to pursue success at all costs and rationalize that the end justifies the means. "Making it happen" is one's ever-present background music. Hustling becomes one's way of life. To me, hustling has connotations of relentless toil. Is there a better way of attaining success? What is God's opinion of success? What does God say about success?

Not surprisingly God's view on success is dramatically different from that of the mainstream. I've found Psalm 37 to be rich in delineating what God will do for His children, and what His children should and should not do. I'll use the NET Bible translation (I bolded and underlined Psalm 37:23 for emphasis) for this compilation:

Do:

- Psalm 37:3 Trust in the Lord and do what is right! Settle in the land and maintain your integrity!
- Psalm 37:4 Then you will take delight in the Lord,
- Psalm 37:5 Commit your future to the Lord! Trust in him and he will act on your behalf.
- Psalm 37:7 Wait patiently for the Lord! Wait confidently for him!
- Psalm 37:21...but the godly show compassion and are generous.
- Psalm 37:26 All day long he shows compassion and lends to others, and his children are blessed.
- Psalm 37:27 Turn away from evil! Do what is right!
- Psalm 37:29 The godly will possess the land and will dwell in it permanently.
- Psalm 37:30 The godly speak wise words and promote justice.
- Psalm 37:31 The law of their God controls their thinking; their feet do not slip.
- Psalm 37:34 Rely on the Lord! Obey his commands!

- Psalm 37:37 Take note of the one who has integrity! Observe the godly! For the one who promotes peace has a future.

Don't:

- Psalm 37:1 Do not fret when wicked men seem to succeed! Do not envy evildoers!
- Psalm 37:7…Do not fret over the apparent success of a sinner, a man who carries out wicked schemes!
- Psalm 37:8 Do not be angry and frustrated! Do not fret! That only leads to trouble!

God's Actions:

- Psalm 37:4…he will answer your prayers.
- Psalm 37:5…he will act on your behalf.
- Psalm 37:6 He will vindicate you in broad daylight, and publicly defend your just cause.
- Psalm 37:17…but the Lord sustains the godly.
- Psalm 37:18 The Lord watches over the innocent day by day and they possess a permanent inheritance.
- **<u>Psalm 37:23 The Lord grants success to the one whose behavior he finds commendable.</u>**
- Psalm 37:24…for the Lord holds his hand.
- Psalm 37:28 For the Lord promotes justice, and never abandons his faithful followers.

- Psalm 37:33 But the Lord does not surrender the godly, or allow them to be condemned in a court of law.
- Psalm 37:39-40 But the Lord delivers the godly; he protects them in times of trouble. The Lord helps them and rescues them; he rescues them from evil men and delivers them, for they seek his protection.

God grants His kind of success, godly success, to His children in the measure that they love, trust, and obey Him and His ways. Accordingly, this book's focus upon godly success is derived from God's Word, which declares that God has a good plan for each of His children. *What good news!* It's important to know and believe this as you journey towards realization of your dreams, often in the face of challenges of all types.

I've particularly needed this revelation to exercise faith in the face of fear. To build my faith, I meditate upon God's thoughts for my future that are best summarized (I added italics for emphasis) in various translations of Jeremiah 29:11 as shown below:

- Jeremiah 29:11 (CEV): I will *bless you* with a future filled with *hope* – a future of *success*, not of suffering.
- Jeremiah 29:11 (NIV): "For I know the plans I have for you", declares The Lord, "plans to *prosper* you and not to harm you, plans to give you *hope* and a *future.*"
- Jeremiah 29:11 (King James Version): for I know the thoughts that I think toward you, saith The Lord, thoughts of *peace*, and not of evil, to give you an *expected end*.
- Jeremiah 29:11 (AMP): For I know the thoughts and plans that I have for you, says The Lord, thoughts and

plans for *welfare* and *peace* and not for evil, to give you *hope* in your final outcome.
- Jeremiah 29:11 (Good News Bible): I alone know the plans I have for you, plans to bring you *prosperity* and not disaster, plans to bring about the future you hope for.
- Jeremiah 29:11 (Message Bible): I know what I'm doing. I have it all planned out – plans *to take care of you*, not abandon you, plans to give you the future you hope for.
- Jeremiah 29:11 (NET): 'For I know what I have planned for you', says The Lord, 'I have plans to *prosper* you, not to harm you. I have plans to give you a future filled with *hope*.'

The center or core of Jeremiah 29:11 is God's declaration that He has specific and deliberate thoughts and plans for His children's future. Features of God's plans for His children include prosperity, caretaking, and opening of doors. The wording of the actual Scriptures proclaims God's active engagement in securing good on behalf of His children. ***He is definitely for His children!***

Foundation: God has A Good Plan for My Life!

Before diving into specifics of how to apply Biblical strategies for godly success, it's important to lay the foundation these strategies are derived from. God's Word, the Bible, is the foundation. I've found it helpful to think of the Bible as God speaking to His children across the span of time, sharing His love and provision for them. I typically personalize God's Word, putting my name in the place of words like "you" to reinforce the concept of God speaking directly to me from His living, all powerful Word. God loves His children with an everlasting, faithful love that has no limits. I'm encouraged when I consider the breadth of His love and provision for His children. I summarize significant realizations as:

I. I am here for specific purposes.
  A. God knew me before I was born. Jeremiah 1:5 records, "I knew you before I formed you in your mother's womb" (NLT).
  B. I am unique – I am fearfully and wonderfully made by God. King David shared in Psalm 139:14, "I praise you because I am fearfully and wonderfully made; your works are wonderful, I know that full well" (NIV).
  C. God loves me as I am and will evolve to be. In Jeremiah 31:3, God declares, "I have loved you with an everlasting love; I have drawn you with unfailing kindness" (NIV).
  D. God created me to perform specific work. In Ephesians 2:10, God reveals, "For we are God's handiwork, created in Christ Jesus to do good works, which God prepared in advance for us to do" (NIV).

II. God empowers me to fulfill my life purposes.

God knows me completely and I can be completely real with Him. I am an open book before God – nothing is hidden from Him. So why is it tempting to hide from The One who loves me unfailingly, particularly when I've fallen short? The parable of the Prodigal Son is such a loving picture of how God loves us, despite our shortcomings. His arms are wide open, eager to embrace us and restore fellowship. In different seasons of my life, I've acted like the younger son and the older son. Yes, I'm able to admit it. Many times, I've demanded my way and have taken off on my own. Other times I've taken on a martyr's complex, acting like a servant though knowing I'm a daughter. Despite my actions, God has always been patient and compassionate towards me. Loving me beyond my faults, he saw His child…precious, lovable, and special. I continually marvel that I am a joint heir with Jesus and that Jesus loves me as fully as God my Father. I'm learning to live as a member of God's royal family, secure in the knowledge that God's love never fails and God will never forsake me.

I love the beauty of the poetry of Psalms. Indulge me as I share my thoughts of God's advocacy of us in my own form of poetry:

> *God wants the best for me*…choosing my purpose **before** my design.
>
> *God loves me unconditionally*…as demonstrated on Calvary.
>
> *God's presence settles me*…with God on my side whom shall I fear?
>
> *God's power protects me.*… The Omnipotent One protects my very life.
>
> *God's provision sustains me*…The All Sufficient One meets my every need.
>
> *God's faithfulness humbles me*…He loves unfailingly.
>
> *God's love frees me*…I am cherished beyond my comprehension.

III. God is an ever-present Help throughout the seasons of my life.

God cares about every aspect of my life. What do you feel when you consider that God has numbered every hair on your head? The Bible records how God takes care of the sparrows and reassures us of His care for us. He cares so much that He doesn't want us to be burdened with our cares. We're told to cast our cares on Jesus for He cares for us and in exchange we'll experience peace that transcends all understanding (see 1 Peter 5:7 and Philippians 4:6-7). What a supreme exchange!

> When I'm afraid, *He is resolute* (Psalm 56:3).
>
> When I'm uncertain, *He is steadfast* (Psalm 69:13).
>
> When I feel abandoned, *He is my comforter* (Psalm 27:10).
>
> When I'm in need, *He is my source* (Philippians 4:19).
>
> When I'm sad, *He is my joy* (Psalm 30:11).
>
> When I'm discouraged, *He is my confidence and lifter of my head* (Psalm 3:3).

IV. God freely shares His wisdom for living purposefully.

I'm particularly appreciative of Proverbs as a book of God's Word devoted to giving instructions for godly success and purposeful living. I've found *Proverbs: Wisdom from Above*, The Passion Translation, which Dr. Brian Simmons translated from original Hebrew and Greek texts, to be profoundly insightful and rich for self-study. I'll refer to *Proverbs: Wisdom from Above*, The Passion Translation in the takeaway sections of subsequent chapters.

CHAPTER 1

Keep First Things First!

According to John 1:1-3, "In the beginning was the Word, and the Word was with God, and the Word was God. He was with God in the beginning. Through him all things were made; without him nothing was made that has been made."

Today it's so easy to get caught in the crossfire of so many competing priorities. Whether at home or at work, there seems to be so much to do at all times. Even though we know that all things aren't equally important, our actions seem to prove otherwise. Compounded with the pervasive nature of technology, we seem to move and live in environments without boundaries. So how do we decide what's most important in setting our priorities for the day? We know that time is a finite resource. There are no do-overs or rollovers. With each new day, we have 86, 400 seconds - no more and no less. Each person has the same allocation, regardless of gender, ethnicity, country of origin, etc.

So what do we do? James 1:5 says, "If any of you lacks wisdom, you should ask God, who gives generously to all without finding fault, and it will be given to you". In terms of prioritizing, God says, "But seek first the kingdom of God and his righteousness, and all these things will be added to you" (Matthew 6:33, ESV).

So what does that mean for us today? Similar to the concept of tithing, give God the first fruits of your day. I've come to approach this in the following manner each morning:

A. **Initiate conversation with God.** I check in with God first, which means that I communicate with God in reading His Word and communing with him in prayer and quiet time. I want to start my day knowing that my connection with God is clear. I want to experience anew the security of being within his circle of protection and blessing. I don't know what the day holds for me, but He does. So I check in with Him to hear from Him and be prepared for the day. I believe the surest foundation for living is His love. Knowing that I am unconditionally loved by The Most High God is transformational. God is love and His love never fails. He, The Omnipotent, Omniscient, and Omnipresent One is with and for me...I have no thing or no one to fear. I can face the day with confidence, flowing with and in God's grace.

B. **Invest time in listening to God.** We're so used to having one-way conversations with God. We talk and talk, sharing our petitions, concerns, etc. And when we're finished with what we have to say, we're quick to end our time of togetherness. Have you ever had a telephone conversation with someone like that? She may ask how you're doing (typically out of habit) and let you get out a few words before she hijacks the conversation. From that point on, it's an exercise in being an extra in The World According to ___. With rapid fire speed, she dumps her woes or triumphs. Between her rare pauses to take a breath, you attempt to change the subject - to no avail. Once she's unloaded her thoughts (which often takes much longer than you wanted to spend in listening), she's ready to end the conversation. Irritated at the expenditure of time and now feeling out of sorts by her conversation, you glare at the phone accusingly and vow not to be ambushed by her again. Bottom line, the engagement with her is extremely dissatisfying because you feel taken advantage of. Do we similarly take advantage of God? We're quick to "dial Him up" when in need, but often give Him a busy signal when He attempts to speak…possibly leaving Him saying, "Can you hear me now?" In fact, we're encouraged to "Be still…" (Psalm 46:10). That goes beyond our physical movements and includes our thoughts and words. Remember that God is spirit. This means that He speaks to us in our spirits and not our minds (which are part of our souls). In quieting our mouths and minds and listening for God in our spirits, we are in the position to hear from God.

What does He want us to do for Him this day? After all, we need to know His priorities to advance His kingdom as He desires. He is in the lead and not the other way around. A sure way of knowing that I've managed my day faithfully is knowing and following His lead for that day. Why is this important? Because we are stewards of His resources and are accountable to Him for our management of His resources.

Takeaways

Keep: Maintain and be consistent in.

First Things First: Highest importance and comes before all others in order.

Proverbs TPT reference:

> Before you do anything,
>
> Put your trust totally in God and not in yourself,
>
> Then every plan you make will succeed. (Proverbs 16:3)

CHAPTER 2
Set the Atmosphere!

In thinking about atmosphere, I consider the dimensions of spirit, soul, and body. These three are interrelated and proper alignment of each with God's good thoughts toward us is powerful.

Spirit: Putting God first in maintaining mindfulness of His way of doing and being right puts one in great position for taking on the day. In this daily download with God, we again experience His awesome exchange. His love, strength, protection, faithfulness, and peace displace our fear, weaknesses, vulnerabilities, and anxieties...*if* we will trust Him.

Soul: Renewing our minds to God's way of doing and being right reinforces peacefulness within us. Too often, we play tapes in our minds of false beliefs that hinder us from becoming all that God created us to be. Importantly, our minds strive to manifest as reality those images and thoughts that we consciously and unconsciously meditate upon. To give my mind images (word pictures) that are consistent with how God thinks about me, I speak out loud the following words over myself each morning (similar to the scenes in the movie *The Help*):

Blessed! Loved! Protected! Empowered! Healed! Favored! Faithful!

Beautiful! Peaceful! Overcomer! Victor! More than a conqueror!

What you say to yourself matters. The Bible reveals "for as he thinks in his heart, so is he" (Proverbs 23:7, AMP). I choose to believe what God says about me and to speak His Word over my life. My favorite declarations and truths from God's Word include:

- I am God's child for I am born again of the incorruptible seed of the word of God. (1 Peter 1:23)
- I am redeemed from the curse of the law of sin and death. (1 Peter 1:18–19; Galatians 3:13)
- I am free from condemnation. (Romans 8:1)
- I am healed by the stripes of Jesus. (1 Peter 2:24; Isaiah 53:5)
- I am chosen and dearly loved by Christ. (Ephesians 1:4; 1 Peter 2:9)
- I have been given a spirit of power, love, and a sound mind. (2 Timothy 1:7)
- I declare that through God, the battle is already won! (1 Samuel 17:47)
- I believe God has sent his word and it will not return void! (Isaiah 55:11)
- I expect God's mercy and grace on me today! (Lamentations 3:22–23)

- I expect God's favor and blessings on me today! (Psalm 5:12; Jeremiah 29:11)
- I believe God has given me His abundant life. (John 10:10)
- The Lord is my shepherd and I do not want. (Psalm 23:1)
- The blessings of the Lord make me truly rich and He adds no sorrow with it. (Proverbs 10:22)
- I delight myself in the Lord and He gives me the desires of my heart. (Psalm 37:4)
- Do not be anxious about anything, but in every situation, by prayer and petition, with thanksgiving, present your requests to God. And the peace of God, which transcends all understanding, will guard your hearts and your minds in Christ Jesus. (Philippians 4:6-7)

Always remember that you have the power to control what you let into your mind and what you subsequently think upon. Be your own advocate and build your self-esteem and faith upon the sure foundation of God's Word.

Body: Whether I'm at home or in my professional setting, I make sure to set up my physical environments in ways that affirm me. That means I create my spaces so that they're filled with things I like and that inspire me. I like spaces that are clean, orderly, colorful, and inspirational. I also cherish healthy green plants, pictures of the beach or items taken from the beach, pictures of people I love, air fragrances that remind me of the tropics or the beach, luscious fruit in stylish containers, and vision boards with powerful words and images that inspire me to higher levels of accomplishment. I'm very intentional in creating environments that inspire my best work.

Take responsibility for creating powerful atmospheres that echo God's wonderful, affirming thoughts towards you! I do understand that your amount of control over your physical work spaces may be limited…still, do the most you can…it's time well invested…

Takeaways

Set: Understand yourself and choose to establish conditions that bring out your best abilities.

The Atmosphere: Exercise authority in the environments you occupy.

Proverbs TPT reference:

Eyes that focus on what is beautiful

Bring joy to the heart, (Proverbs 15:30)

CHAPTER 3

Be Grateful!

I recall having lunch with a group of high school students as part of an outreach activity. Leaders gave box lunches to each student. Each box lunch was identical...a sandwich, bag of potato chips, big cookie, and juice. As the students munched noisily, one voice rose over the din. It was the voice of a teen I'll call Kim. She noticed that I hadn't opened my box lunch and she asked me for my cookie. I looked at Kim quizzically, for she still had her half eaten cookie in her hand. She hadn't eaten her sandwich or any of the other lunch items. "Why do you want my cookie?" I asked. "You haven't eaten what you have!" Stonily, Kim looked at me and declared, "I want more!" I told her to eat her entire meal and if there were leftover box lunches, she might be able to get another cookie. Displeased with my answer, Kim turned to another adult and demanded, "Can I have your cookie?" I just stared at her incredulously. What was driving her to demand more before finishing what she had?

Why was I irritated by her audacity? Was it her tone, sense of entitlement, or something else? As I think about the encounter now, I think her actions are representative of a lot of us. We have, but we want more. What we have, we judge to be insufficient. In our homes, we have TV and Internet that incessantly spur us on to get more. Images flash before us in living color and high definition that show others that seem to have it all... more money, power, fame, status, beauty, youth, and privilege. Our communities provide ready opportunities for comparison. Keeping up with the Joneses is a typical endeavor. In our workplaces, competition is the norm. With mainstream's consciousness of scarcity, thoughts and behaviors inconsistent with gratitude abound. Perceived threats are everywhere...like the TV show *Survivor* run amuck.

It's easy to be so caught up in the journey of becoming that one forgets the beauty present in today. To me, it seems quite ironic that we most overlook the very things that are most important in the long term. How often have we rejected time with a loved one in favor of pursuing a job prospect or commitment that has no meaning for us a year later? How often have we promised ourselves to spend more time with an aged relative only to run out of time to be with them?

You've probably heard of gratitude journals and know various ways of expressing gratitude to God for what you have in your life. God is the Giver of all good gifts and it's only right to thank Him for all that He's done for us. Sometimes it's easier than other times to be grateful. When things are going good and we feel good, it seems easier to be grateful or does it? Do we, in the good times, take God's goodness for granted and become distracted with other things? What about during the hard times? When you feel that you've been ambushed and knocked out by challenging situations, how can you be grateful - especially when God seems distant and friends are few? My question to you is, "Has God changed?" God's Word reveals that God does not change (see James 1:17).

Before even considering your situation, how about first focusing upon who God is? Remember that God is the Omniscient, Omnipotent, and Omnipresent One. No problem we can face is greater than Him. He is not fretting about what to do in your situation. Review of God's Word reveals how He has already defeated every foe you can face. Knowing God's provision is integral to overcoming your circumstances. However, the battles we face typically present themselves in physical forms, yet they are of spiritual origin. This means we have to put on and skillfully use our spiritual armor. Consequently, love, faith, and action are critical enablers of appropriating God's Word and having Him meet your every need. Stated differently, the degree to which we believe and act on God's Word is the degree to which we will experience the power of His Word...this is directly correlated to Luke 6:38 that states, "For with the measure you use, it will be measured to you."

As you stand in faith on God's Word to manifest in your situation, what do you do? Fear not. Don't worry. Think on those things that are true, noble, right, pure, lovely, and admirable (see Philippians 4:8). Express thankfulness to God for His faithfulness. Keep your focus on God and His Word. Remember Peter and his experience of walking on the water. As we focus on God's Word, we maintain our position of dominion over that which would try to overwhelm us...it may look and feel intimidating, but the truth is that it is a defeated foe. With Jesus' resurrection, He made an open show (see Colossians 2:15) of the enemy and all of the enemy's works, which collectively are under the curse of sin and death. Jesus has redeemed us from the curse of the law of sin and death and set us free to the law of the spirit of life in Christ Jesus. The curse has no power, authority, and place over those who've accepted salvation purchased through Jesus' crucifixion on the cross. The knowledge and belief of this are critical as reinforced in Revelation 12:11. What you know and believe matters and really is a matter of life and death.

So, how can we be grateful despite our current situations? I recommend having a tight grasp on God's truth. He loves us; will never forsake us; has a good plan for our lives; has sacrificed Jesus to save us and restore us to life and dominion; has empowered us with His Word, the name of Jesus, the presence of the Holy Spirit; and angelic protection. Yes, we will encounter tribulations in our lives, but the good news is that we are overcomers through what God has already done and given us. The question becomes will we take our place as His royal children and act in the power, authority, and dominion He has given us?

God will not and does not lie. His Word is truth, life, and healing. He is the All Sufficient One who meets your every need in His riches and glory in Christ Jesus (see Philippians 4:19). If you're in need, go to His Word and learn His solution for your problem. He is extravagantly generous and eager to bless His children. Your deliverance is as close as your quality decision to know, believe, receive, and act on His Word. I believe that's something to be quite grateful about!!

Takeaways

Be: Determine, regardless of circumstances, to have a particular mindset.

Grateful: Daily take time to thank God and remind yourself of His grace and mercy bestowed on you.

Proverbs TPT reference:

> Everything seems to go wrong
>
> When you feel weak and depressed.
>
> But when you choose to be cheerful,
>
> Every day will bring you
>
> More and more joy and fullness. (Proverbs 15:15)

CHAPTER 4

Do It Today!

All right, now that you've had your time in fellowship with God and know what is important to Him for you to do today, you're ready to plan out how you intend to invest your time for the day. Yes, I'm talking about your "To Do" list. My take on the "To Do" list is a bit different. I begin with the intention to list the least number of items on my "To Do" list, choosing instead to list those items that provide the best return for my investment. This concept is known as the Pareto principle, which basically states that 20% of the things that you do will yield 80% of the desired results. To be able to leverage this properly, that means that I have to understand what are those tasks that will really give me the best return on my time. This provides me a very useful dividing line, separating the "Must Do" items from the "Like To Do" items.

Another tactic I use in prioritizing my "To Do" actions (I say actions instead of tasks because for me tasks has negative connotations - sounds like drudgery) is to first do the items that I like the least…for whatever reasons. I prefer to tackle my least preferred actions when I'm at my best and when I finish them, it's such a lift. I move on to my other actions with greater enjoyment. This approach also helps me in maintaining focus. As I look at the items, I estimate how much time I should allocate to their completion. So as I go through the day, I monitor my progress, comparing my estimated and actual completion times.

Knowing that life happens, I also allow buffers within my estimates so that I can readily respond to unforeseen demands on my time. At the same time, my time consciousness helps me to avoid unnecessary time robbers, such as drive-by conversations that others would like to have via the phone or office visits. My preference is to schedule meetings and optimize email communications for capturing information that can't be readily remembered. Nonetheless, I believe in the goodness of walking around and engaging my team members. These engagements build rapport while also getting business done on specific actions. Also, sometimes it's just better to talk to someone face-to-face than to send an email message that could be easily misinterpreted.

This time management approach is grounded in diligence and discipline, which are character traits that God's Word speaks of highly. We are stewards of God's resources and He expects us to be diligent. Proverbs is quite blunt in its denouncement of laziness and procrastination. I remember one day reading Proverbs 6:9 after I had gotten up real late in the morning and hearing, "How long will you stay in bed, you slacker? When will you get up from your sleep?"

Ouch! God's Word is a double edged sword…dividing soul and spirit (see Hebrews 4:12)… imagine my discomfort. Though the morning was spent, I resolved to make my afternoon count. Please don't misunderstand my point in this situation. Yes, rest is important, but in this situation I was simply being lazy (and not sleeping in due to rest needs from earlier hard work). God and I knew that I had been slack…

Another dimension of my lethargy was procrastination. It's easy to put off until tomorrow what can be done today. Again, God warns us to act differently. Proverbs shares an interesting observation,

> "I went past the field of a sluggard, past the vineyard of someone who has no sense; thorns had come up everywhere, the ground was covered with weeds, and the stone wall was in ruins. I applied my heart to what I observed and learned a lesson from what I saw: A little sleep, a little slumber, a little folding of the hands to rest – and poverty will come on you like a thief and scarcity like an armed man" (Proverbs 24:30-34).

Procrastination is a thief, robbing you of your valuable time. Though certain seasons of our lives seem like they will never end, we really only have a short amount of time to work. Night is coming when no man will work. If your work only impacted you, the consequences of procrastination and inaction would be minimized. But that's not the case. God has created you with gifts that others need. Burying your gift like the fearful steward in the parable of the talents will yield similar rebuke. God expects us to gain increases on His investments in us. We are accountable to Him for what we do. Further, our stewardship of His resources has temporal and eternal consequences.

If fear and/or self-limiting beliefs are keeping you from doing what you know you should do, I recommend you go straight to God's Word. His Word has the healing virtue that can restore and uplift you to move out in faith. His love and support will displace the fear. See Him in His Word, telling you, "Come." You can do what He has created you to do. "Take up your bed and walk!"

Takeaways
Do: Take action.
It: Identify the specific actions most integral to completion of your goals.
Today: Now is the time to do what God has led you to do. Do it with a sense of urgency because someone is counting on you!
Proverbs TPT reference:

> "Professional work habits
>
> Prevent poverty from becoming your
>
> Permanent business partner."
>
> And, "If you put off until tomorrow the work
>
> You could do today,
>
> Tomorrow never seems to come." (Proverbs 24:33-34)

CHAPTER 5

Complete Something!

Do you have a track record of completing what you start? Why is it important to finish what you start? Let's take a step backwards and reflect on our behaviors. Would you patronize a professional that doesn't complete her work? Who would pay for an incomplete hair style; knowingly drive over an unfinished bridge; buy an unfinished book; ride on a "nearly" finished plane; or pay for a half-baked cake? Not me! Yes, there are varying levels of risk in these examples, but the principle is constant. Completion is a critical measure of performance and expectation. In a hiring recruiter's mind, there's quite a distinction between a job candidate who has taken coursework towards degree completion and a job candidate who has completed coursework and possesses a degree.

Completion requires commitment, focus, and time. That's why it's so important to identify those actions that are most aligned with your God-led goals and invest your time in completing them. Their completion is essential to your goal accomplishment. This phase of **execution is the power twin to goal setting**.

A key to completing goals that appear intimidating is to break the goals into smaller achievable steps. These steps can be broken down into discrete daily actions to include in your "To Do" list. Suppose I set a goal of saving $1,500 in one year. How could I make this goal less intimidating through consistent action? Well, I'd calculate how much money I needed to save each month to meet my goal in 12 months. Dividing $1,500 by 12 reveals I need to save $125 each month for 12 months. Taking it further, subsequent calculations reveal I need to save $31.25 each week for 48 weeks, which may still be a bit of a stretch. However, if I calculate what I'd need to save each work day (assuming a 5 day work week), I find that I just need to save $6.25 for 240 work days. Now, I just have to find daily work day savings of $6.25. I have several options, such as brown bagging lunch, or forgoing breakfast coffee and pastry, or forgoing afternoon snacks. I could do this! I could even gain healthier eating habits while reaching my savings goal!

Commitment to the daily action of saving $6.25 will get me to my desired goal of $1,500 in savings. Furthermore, this consistent action is building my confidence in my ability to achieve my goals. With this track record of success with my savings goal, I could move on to loftier goals, knowing I have the discipline and resolve to persevere and reach my goals.

If perfectionism is a barrier to completion for you, I recommend you accept the concept, "Done is better than perfect". It took me some time to embrace this…mainly because I thought the statement was condoning substandard work. Not so. Chandler Bolt, Co-Founder and CEO of Self-Publishing School explained it as doing good work as you complete the various phases (or steps) of the action. For example, consider book writing. As an author, I have to fight against self-editing my work so much that

I can never get beyond writing my first chapter. Instead, it's more advantageous for me to write a good first draft of each chapter and compile a complete first draft of my book. With the first draft of the book completed, I then have the luxury of going back and editing the various chapters at will. Notice the advantage completion of the book's first draft gives me...I am tremendously closer to book completion and launch, which is my goal.

Another strategy for overcoming perfectionism is to adopt a "satisficer" mindset that Dr. Barry Schwartz coined as a hybrid of the words "satisfy" and "suffice". Valorie Burton, renowned personal and executive coach, explains a "satisficer" as one who determines the minimum standard for satisfaction with an action and determines beforehand to select the first action that meets this standard. This approach yields efficiency in allowing you to complete actions acceptably and move on to other actions requiring your attention. Looking back, I see that I could have made great use of this approach, particularly with typical administrative data submissions to my higher headquarters. Instead of spending hours in correcting and proofreading subordinate data inputs to provide perfect submissions, I could charge my managers with ensuring the data was accurate and legible and forwarding the data as required. I could then be free to focus my attention on efforts that truly required my direct involvement and guidance. Every administrative submission wasn't of equal importance. Perfectionism was counterproductive to my ability to complete the "Must Do" actions of my "To Do" lists. Though I was completing actions every work day, the completion of my "Must Do" actions was moving progressively later in the day as I engaged in completion of other's "Must Do" actions...probably explains why my work days were so long...

Now that I know better, I do better. With God's guidance, I now consistently choose meaningful goals in my professional and personal life. Along with their identification, I commit to daily movement towards their completion. Discernment guides me in being a "satisficer". All actions aren't equally important and surely all aren't deserving of huge amounts of thought, concentration, and time. Selecting a pair of shoes and choosing an investment plan probably require significantly different levels of analysis and research…*I'm just saying…*

Takeaways
Complete: Finish it! Commit to completing that which is necessary and important…know that completion positions you for greater advancement, trust, opportunity, and success.
Something: Be intentional…don't do something by default and/or just because it's easy…take a step every day that gets you closer to your goals…don't sell yourself short.
Proverbs TPT reference:

> A passive person won't even complete a project,
>
> But a passionate person makes good use
>
> Of his time, wealth, and energy. (Proverbs 12:27)

CHAPTER 6

Connect Meaningfully!

No Man Is An Island

No man is an island,

No man stands alone,

Each man's joy is joy to me,

Each man's grief is my own…

- Joan Baez, *Baptism: A Journey Through Our Time*

If we want godly success, it follows that we should be closely linked to God to understand His way of being and doing right as well as being empowered by Him to do things His way. Isolation and separation are not characteristics of God's way of being and doing right. His triune being gives first evidence of His prioritization of interdependence. God is three in one: God, Jesus, and the Holy Spirit. God created mankind to have three elements: spirit, soul, and body. Revelation of the interdependence between God and mankind provides understanding of the connections between God and His children.

Jesus is the bridge between God and mankind. Those who accept salvation provided by Jesus' sacrifice on the cross are God's children. His children comprise the church (the body) whose head is Jesus. The church is likened to a body (see 1 Corinthians 12:27) in explanation of how God's children relate as members of one body:

> Even so the body is not made up of one part but of many. Now if the foot should say, "Because I am not a hand, I do not belong to the body," it would not for that reason stop being part of the body...But God has put the body together... that its parts should have equal concern for each other. If one part suffers, every part suffers with it; if one part is honored, every part rejoices with it.
> (1Corinthians 12:14-15, 24-26).

For each member to function as it should, it has to remain connected to Jesus. In verses four through five of chapter fifteen of the book of John, Jesus reveals Himself as the True Vine in sharing,

> Remain in me, as I also remain in you. No branch can bear fruit by itself; it must remain in the vine. Neither can you bear fruit unless you remain in me. I am the vine; you are the branches. If you remain in me and I in you, you will bear much fruit; apart from me you can do nothing.

Can you think of another example in God's word that shows the power of connection? I think of marriage. Especially when I consider God's insight that, "Though one may be overpowered, two can defend themselves. A cord of three strands is not quickly broken" (Ecclesiastes 4:12). This threefold cord manifests when Christ comes into the midst of two united believers. Remember Jesus declaring, "For where two or three gather in my name, there am I with them" (Matthew 18:20). Union is powerful. Two is better than one and, of course, many surpasses two.

This discussion raises an important question to consider. What and whom am I connected to? Using the analogy of "eye" gates and "ear" gates, who and what am I giving access to my spirit, soul, and body? What am I primarily experiencing in my life? Chapter Five of Galatians clearly delineates between the fruit of the Spirit and works of the flesh. Not surprisingly the two are opposites. Fruit of the Spirit include love, peace, faith, and self-control, whereas works of the flesh include hatred, strife, dissensions, and impurity. Be a fruit inspector…what are you producing based upon your associations? You're likely familiar with the saying, "Birds of a feather flock together", which is predated by the wisdom of Proverbs that shares many insights, such as "Do not make friends with a hot-tempered person, do not associate with one easily angered, or you may learn their ways and get yourself ensnared" (Proverbs 22:24-25).

So far, this discussion has focused upon us being recipients or objects of connection. However, we're also agents of connection. Again, we need to take on the role of fruit inspectors. How are we investing our time? Are we making meaningful connections for God? What positive differences are we making in advancing God's kingdom? Remembering that God created me to fulfill specific purposes, my connections need to be intentional and strategic. After all, I know that I have to give an account of my stewardship to

God. Furthermore, I've found that my greatest joys have stemmed from doing what God created me to do... which usually involved me enthusiastically supporting and serving others. Conversely, isolation saps my joy and energy. Isolation or connection, it's your choice. I highly recommend meaningful (that is godly) connection and assert it could become a matter of life and death.

Takeaways

Connect: Who and what do I feed on? How much of my daily diet is God's life-giving Word and His work? How much of my diet is the fast food of self-centered pursuits? What impacts are my diet having upon my current quality of life, destiny, and eternity?

Meaningfully: How well do my associations align with God's values and priorities? What do I need to do to be true to who He has called me to be?

Proverbs TPT reference:

> Sharing words of wisdom
>
> Are satisfying to your inner being.
>
> It encourages you to know that you've
>
> Changed someone else's life. (Proverbs 18:20)

CHAPTER SEVEN

Do Something Good!

What is it about doing something affirming that makes you feel good? Whether you do something good for yourself or others, the act of doing good is profound. You find yourself considering other things you could do that build upon your initial action of goodness. At my busiest, a bath is a luxury...

Big Luxury

I sit on my couch and pick up the remote control.

What do I want to see? I ask myself.

Comedy? Drama? News? Sports? I don't know – I begin to channel surf.

Skip over, linger, skim, stare – whatever I do, it's my call.

No one else to say Stop! I want to see that – no, I don't want to see that!

I don't have to negotiate, play nice, or feign interest.

It may seem small to you, but to me it's a ***big luxury***...

A little bit later, I go to the bathroom and shut the door.

In this space, I'm surrounded by things I adore.

I turn the faucet and hot water leaps out.

I jerk my hands back, then add bubble bath.

White, soapy bubbles caress my skin as I sink to my tub's depths...*Ahh*...

I inhale the spicy scent of ginger with faint lavender undertones.

Thank you, Lord for these precious moments to be alone.

At this moment, I'm free - no worries.

In this moment, simple pleasures transcend all stresses.

What can I do to make more of my day more like this?

Is this what it means to enter God's rest?

Yes, only in God do I find peace that surpasses all understanding.

Knowing He'll never leave or forsake me, I'm capable of standing.

No matter the issue, God's Word is clear...I'm often exhorted not to fear.

God loves me! Yes, He's with me!

A smile begins inside and quickly bursts forth.

Yes, God loves me unconditionally and empowers me faithfully.

Outwardly perfumed and inwardly renewed, I exit my bathroom.

Better than the delights of the bath experience is my talk with myself.

Time alone is all it took – maybe small to you, but to me, it's a ***big luxury***!

-By Dr. Stephanie L. Foster, Copyright ©2015

Doing something good for someone else is similarly empowering. I like that it gets me out of my own head and focusing upon what I have that can help someone else. In giving, I gain greater awareness of who God created me to be and where I fit in His big plan. I relearn that my life matters and that others are counting on me to do what I was created to do. These statements may seem lofty, but even at the most basic levels, my connections with others matter. Simple acts of kindness are transformational. A few words of encouragement may override someone's contemplation of suicide. Some dollars may keep someone from resorting to crime to meet basic needs. A stand for justice will give a voice to the invisible. We may not know the impacts of our giving, but God does and He's counting on us to show and share His love with a hurting world. One life does matter and makes a difference.

Let's commit our concerns to God and go about His business in doing good. He'll take care of us and we'll meaningfully impact our world for good!

Takeaways

Do: Choose to take action.
Something: Follow the Holy Spirit's prompting in identifying how to meaningfully give of your resources (talents, time, influence, etc.) to causes beyond your self-interests.
Good: Let your actions declare God's love.
Proverbs TPT reference:

> Generosity brings prosperity,
>
> But withholding from charity
>
> Brings poverty.
>
> Those who live to bless others
>
> Will have blessings heaped upon them,
>
> And the one who pours out his life
>
> To pour out blessings
>
> Will be saturated with favor.
>
> People will curse the businessman with no ethics,
>
> But the one with a social conscience
>
> Receives praise from all.
>
> Living your life seeking what is good for others
>
> Brings untold favor, (Proverbs 11:24-27)

Action Plan

So what does it look like to reconcile these 7 strategies within the context of a single day? I recommend you think of the strategies in terms of consciousness, which allows you to be more intentional in how you invest your time and engage with yourself and others. *Yes*, I said engage with yourself because we engage in self talk throughout the day. Some strategies may seem easier to execute because they more readily align with certain times of the day. To keep things simple, I'll divide the day into three parts: morning, mid-day, and night. I'll use this framework for providing an example of a day of intentional living.

Morning Focus: Pre-emptive Action
Keep First Things First: Invest quality time in fellowshipping with God in prayer, thanksgiving, Bible reading, worship, and quietness. Know God loves you and expect to hear from Him. Determine to obey Him.

Set The Atmosphere: Choose to believe that God is for you and speak His Word over you and your circumstances in faith. Expect God's mercy, grace, favor, blessings, and protection.

Be Grateful: Be appreciative of what you have now. Know that God has a good plan for your life. Determine to trust Him with your life.

Do It Today: Plan your day's activities with sensitivity to the Holy Spirit. Be committed, diligent and intentional in the actions you determine to take. Determine to follow the Holy Spirit's promptings as you go through your day.

Mid-day Focus: Reinforcing Action

Be Grateful: Be appreciative of what you've accomplished and your opportunity to accomplish more before day's end.

Do It Today: Assess your progress with your day's plan ("To Do" List) and refine your plan as needed. Use discernment in reordering actions yet to be completed.

Complete Something: Evaluate your completion status. Acknowledge victories and shortcomings. Devise strategies for overcoming barriers to completion. Commit to completing as many planned actions as possible.

Connect Meaningfully: Don't let the day end without connecting meaningfully with at least one person.

Do Something Good: Do something positive for yourself and someone else. Be as simple or grandiose as you please!

Night Focus: Reconciling Action

Keep First Things First: Close out the day in quality time with God. Share your day with Him and listen for His feedback and guidance. End your day in right standing with Him.

Set The Atmosphere: Expect peaceful sleep (see Proverbs 3:24).

Be Grateful: Meditate on God's goodness and what's right in your life. Sleep peacefully…no worries…

The example above is just that - an example. Be creative in following God's wisdom in your daily life. I purposefully didn't give specific durations for actions, such as fellowshipping with God. Consciousness of His omnipresence frees you to talk to Him anywhere, anytime, and about anything. Flow in His unforced rhythm of grace…He loves you and each day can be your best day - - with Him and those He's blessed you to share your life with!!

Reflections

God, who doesn't change, loves you unconditionally. God loves you - as you were, are, and will be! His words to you are of life, healing, and affirmation: You are dearly loved, valued, wanted, and gifted! According to Jeremiah 29:11 (CEV), His plans are to "…bless you with a future filled with hope – a future of success, not of suffering." Trust your past, present, and future to Him. Godly success can be yours. Your decision to be obedient to God's way of being and doing right will reap harvests of rewards of earthly and eternal consequences. God's Word works. Isaiah 55:11 provides His assurance stating, "so my word that goes out from my mouth: It will not return to Me empty, but will accomplish what I desire and achieve the purpose for which I sent it."

I've come to realize and appreciate God's purpose for me. Blessed, loved, and created intentionally, I choose God's way and to be me…intentionally!

Me…Intentionally!

I'm here for a purpose, God says so.

My life is a gift, I've come to know.

I accept that all won't celebrate me.

Whether they smile or frown, I'll still be free…to be ***me…intentionally!***

I choose to live my best life, governed by God's Word.

I'll live by faith, daring to trust.

What I have is what I need to get what fulfills me.

I'll be my own best friend, kind to myself.

I'll take decisive action on my own behalf.

I'll finish what I start, planning carefully.

If failure emerges, I'm unfazed.

As a teacher, it has a role in my destiny.

The ebb and flow of life, I keep in perspective.

Failure is temporary…success is my natural state of being.

I'll embrace my life as it is today.

Every day I'll take action to draw closer to my goals.

Action by action and step by step, I grow to treasure authenticity.

Who I am and will be are in one accord.

For I've decided once and for all…that I will be *me… intentionally!*

-By Dr. Stephanie L. Foster, Copyright ©2015

References

Baez, J. (1968). No Man Is An Island. *Baptism: A Journey Through Our Time.* Retrieved from www.metrolyrics.com/no-man-is-an-island-lyrics.

Burton, V. (2012). *Successful Women Think Differently* [Kindle Version]. Retrieved from http://www.amazon.com/.

Prayer of Salvation

Throughout this book, I've used phrases such as "God's children". God's children are those who've received Jesus Christ as their Savior. God loves us, demonstrating His matchless love as related in John 3:16, "For God so loved the world that he gave his one and only Son, that whoever believes in him shall not perish but have eternal life". The way to accept salvation is straightforward: "If you declare with your mouth, "Jesus is Lord," and believe in your heart that God raised him from the dead, you will be saved. For it is with your heart that you believe and are justified, and it is with your mouth that you profess your faith and are saved" (Romans 10:9-10).

To accept your salvation, say aloud: *Heavenly Father, in the Name of Jesus, I come before You acknowledging my sins, asking You to forgive all my sins, and desiring to be in right standing with You. The Bible says in Romans 10:9, "If you declare with your mouth, "Jesus is Lord," and believe in your heart that God raised him from the dead, you will be saved". I believe in my heart and confess with my mouth that Jesus is my Savior and Lord of my life! I am saved! Hallelujah! Thank You, Lord, for saving me. In Jesus' Name I pray. Amen!*

About the Author

CEO of *Intentionally Me*, an innovative leadership and professional development company, Dr. Stephanie L. Foster is a Woman of Action whose efforts have earned her the titles of Leader, Educator, Writer, and Entrepreneur. In each capacity, her focus is to provide a nurturing place for others to recognize, affirm, and develop their talents in strategic manners to fulfill their life purposes. In this book, she has shared what she knows to be true. Success is intentional and God's Word is truth.

To learn more about *Intentionally Me*, please view its website at www.intentionallymellc.com.

Made in the USA
Middletown, DE
30 March 2022

63388554R00040